SETTLE & CARLISLE

The Postwar Years

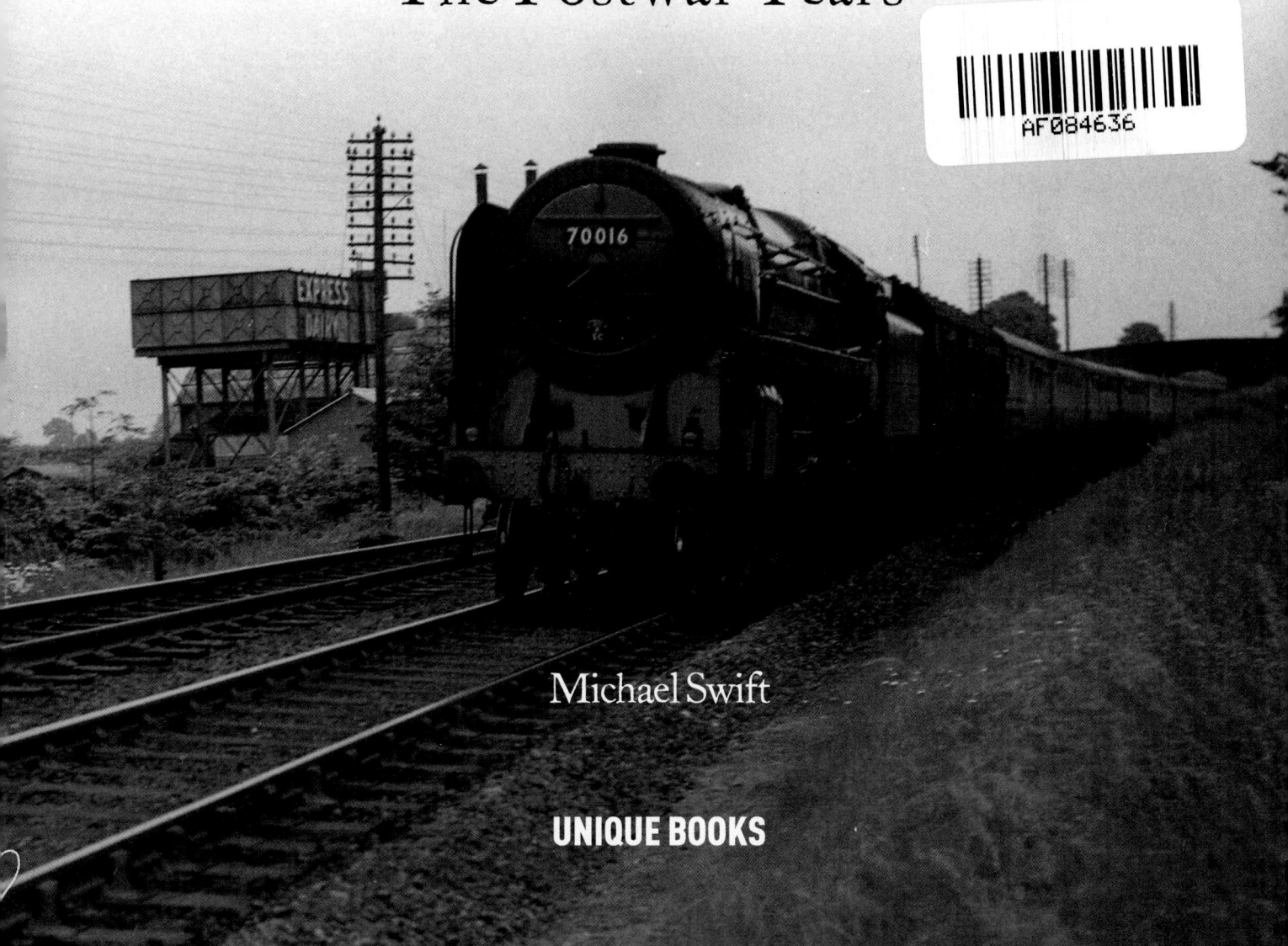

Michael Swift

UNIQUE BOOKS

Front cover: On 6 September 1954, a Down service is pictured approaching Kirkby Stephen station behind a Class 5 4-6-0.
Neil Davenport/Online Transport Archive

Previous page: On 5 July 1951 'Britannia' Class No 70016 *Ariel* is pictured near Appleby with a Down service from Leeds to Glasgow. When recorded here the Pacific was less than a month old – having been delivered new to Holbeck on 18 June – but was to be based in Leeds for only a relatively short period as it was reallocated to Stratford in March 1952. Its subsequent career too the locomotive to the Western Region – between August 1953 and September 1961 – followed by a return to the London Midland; its final shed – Kingmoor – was its base from October 1964 through to withdrawal in August 1967.
Neil Davenport/Online Transport Archive

Settle & Carlisle

Michael Swift

First published in the United Kingdom by Unique Books 2023

© Text: Author 2023
© Photographs: As credited

ISBN: 978 1 913555 14 6

All rights reserved. No part of this book may be reproduced or transmitted in any form or by any means electronic or mechanical, including photocopying, recording or by any information storage without permission from the Publisher in writing. All enquiries should be directed to the Publisher.

A CIP record for this book is available from the British Library

Unique Books is an imprint of Unique Publishing Services Ltd, 3 Merton Court, The Strand, Brighton Marina Village, Brighton BN2 5XY.

www.uniquebooks.pub

Printed in India

A note on the photographs
Many of the illustrations in this book have been drawn from the collection of the Online Transport Archive, a UK-registered charity that was set up to accommodate collections put together by transport enthusiasts who wished to see their precious images secured for the long-term. Further information about the archive can be found at: www.onlinetransportarchive.org or email secretary@onlinetransportarchive.org

INTRODUCTION

THE CONSTRUCTION OF THE LINE from Settle Junction, on the route from Skipton to Morecambe, to Petteril Bridge Junction, on the North Eastern Railway's line from Newcastle to Carlisle, owed much to the railway politics of the late 19th century. Both the London & North Western and Midland railways were keen to exploit the Anglo-Scottish traffic that travelled via Carlisle; whilst the former had its own independent route via Shap, the latter was forced to rely upon its competitor.

The MR's route to the north was via the 'Little North Western' to Ingleton (opened in 1849); there – eventually – an end-on junction with the LNWR was agreed with the latter owning the line north to Low Gill; the Low Gill to Ingleton line opened in 1861. Prior to the agreement, the rival railways had operated separate stations – one to the north and the second to the south of the viaduct – in Ingleton and through passengers had to walk between the two. This was clearly unsatisfactory and, following the agreement, through MR carriages were attached to or detached from LNWR trains. The two stations in Ingleton, however, survived until 1917 when the LNWR station was closed.

The Ingleton line – well-engineered by both railways and double track throughout – represented a useful route but the poor relationship between the LNWR and MR meant that it was never used to its full potential. As a result of these problems, the MR decided that it needed its own independent route to Scotland and, in 1865, started to survey the line. In June 1866 the Royal Assent was given for the construction of the Settle-Carlisle.

Work did not, however, commence immediately; the collapse of the bank Overend, Gurney & Co in May 1866 led to the failure of a number of a number of railway companies and, with pressure from its shareholders, the board of the MR looked at trying to withdraw from the scheme. However, a petition in early 1869 to parliament to authorise abandonment was rejected and the MR was forced to commence work.

Physical construction started in late 1869 and, in many ways, the route was one of the last main lines to be constructed using traditional methods with thousands of navvies employed. Built through some of the most inhospitable countryside in England, the line proved a challenge to its engineer – John Crossley – and to the various contractors employed on it.

The 73-mile line opened to freight traffic in August 1875 with passenger services being introduced on 1 August 1876. Even with major engineering works – the completed line incorporates 22 viaducts and 13 tunnels – some of the gradients were severe; the most famous of these is the 16-mile section from Settle Junction to Blea Moor – known as the 'Long Drag' – where much of the climb is at 1 in 100. The summit at Ais Gill – 1,169ft above sea level – is the highest point reached by any main line railway in England.

The MR's arrival at Carlisle resulted in a third group seeking to capture the traffic between Scotland and England; the MR formed an alliance with the North British, whose extension from Hawick to Carlisle – opened in 1862 – had proved to be a financial disaster until boosted by the through traffic that the MR line offered. From opening through to the Grouping in 1923, the MR sought to improve the competitive position of its route, with a number of cut-off lines either built or planned. In 1923, however, the LNWR and the MR came under common ownership for the first time and increasingly the Settle-Carlisle route was perceived as the poor relation of the two LMS controlled routes from London to Carlisle.

With Nationalisation in 1948 and the continued deterioration of the economics of the railway industry in the 1950s, the position of the Settle-Carlisle line was further eroded. One station on the line – Scotby – had closed during World War 2; four further stations – Cumwhinton, Cotehill, Ormside and Crosby Garrett – were closed in the early to mid-1950s. The first overt threat to the future of the line came with the Beeching report of March 1963; this envisaged the withdrawal of passenger services over the entire route. In the event, however, passenger services – albeit restricted – were retained but all but two of the intermediate stations – Appleby and Settle were the exceptions – were closed on 4 May 1970. Although closed, the stations remained intact and, from 1974, a limited service – 'DalesRail' promoted by the Yorkshire Dales National Park Authority – saw a service to some of the closed stations during summer weekends.

In 1984 BR issued closure notices at the surviving stations. This sparked a major campaign to prevent closure and to encourage the development of the route. Evidence emerged during the process that BR had exaggerated the cost of repairing Ribblehead Viaduct and had diverted traffic away from the route, following a planned 'closure by stealth'. The publicity generated by the proposed closure saw passenger traffic on the route increase five-fold between 1983 and 1989, a process aided by the full reopening of a number of the intermediate stations in 1986. With the then Secretary of State for Transport, Paul Channon, refusing consent for closure on 11 April 1989, work commenced on the long overdue repair to many of the more important structures on the route.

More than three decades after the threat of closure was lifted, the Settle-Carlisle line continues to play an important part in Britain's railway industry and many of the stations and structures along the route have been carefully preserved and restored.

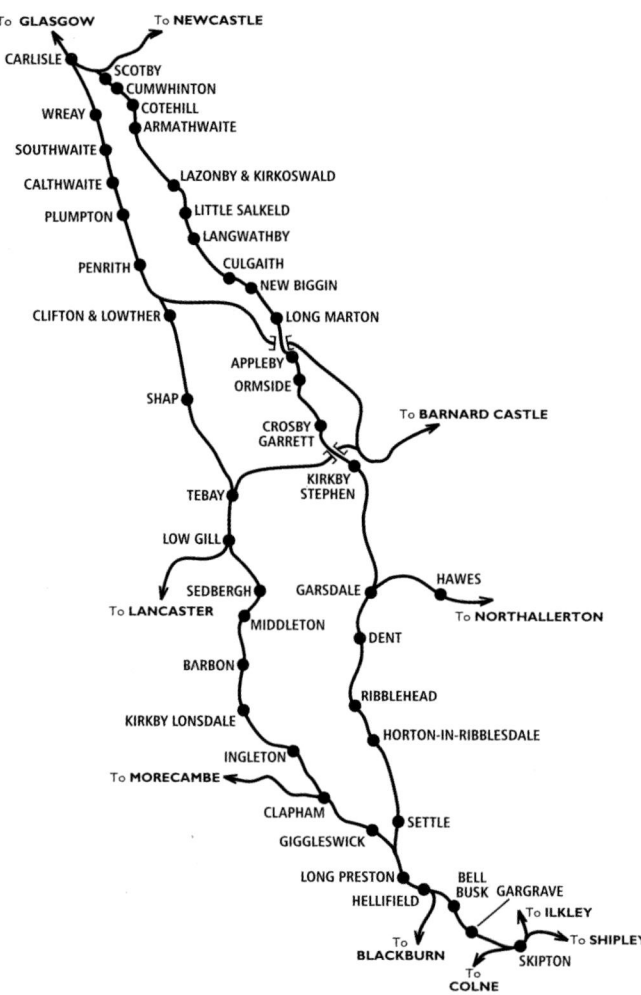

Opposite: The last public timetables to be issued that featured all the surviving intermediate stations was that produced by the LMR for the period from 4 May 1970 to 2 May 1971. However, by the date that the new timetable was due to start, events had overtaken it with the result that a supplement was issued immediately; this stated 'The local service between Skipton and

Leeds to Skipton, Heysham and Carlisle

Miles	Mile	Station		A							B SO		C	D SO			E SO		G SO			H	J MW FX	K
0	—	**LEEDS CITY**	d	02 52					07 55				08 58	09 04		09 20	10 20			10 50		13 00	13 00	13 36
—	—	BRADFORD FORSTER SQUARE	d						*07 55*		08 40		*08c50*			*08c50*	*10 12*		10 40	*10 12*		*12f21*	*12f21*	
10¾	—	SHIPLEY	d			04 40			08 14		08 47		*08c56*			09 40			10 48	11 10		13 19	13 19	
13¾	—	BINGLEY	d						08 21		08 54		*09c03*			09 47			10 55	11 17		13 26	13 26	
17	—	KEIGHLEY	a			04 51			08 27		09 00		09 18	09 28		09 53	10 41		11 01	11 23		13 32	13 32	
		KEIGHLEY	d			05 01			08 28		09 03		09 20	09 29		09 54	10 43		11 03	11 25		13 34	13 34	
26¼	—	**SKIPTON**	a	03 26		05 14			08 40		09 15		09 33			10 06	10 57		11 17	11 37		13 46	13 46	14 08
		SKIPTON	d	03 30					08 42		09 17		09 36			10 08	10 58		11 20	11 39	11 47		13 56	14 11
30	—	GARGRAVE	d													10 15				11 46	11 54			
36¼	—	HELLIFIELD	d													10 26				11 57	12 05			
37¾	—	LONG PRESTON	d													10 29				12 00	12 08			
—	41½	GIGGLESWICK	d													10 36				12 07				The Thames-Clyde Express
—	47½	CLAPHAM (YORKS)	d													10 46				12 17				
—	51½	BENTHAM	d													10 52				12 23				
—	54¾	WENNINGTON	d													10 57				12 28				
—	64¼	**CARNFORTH**	a						09 30		10 02					11 13			12 05	12 42			14 46	
		CARNFORTH	d						09 32		10 04					11 15			12 07	12 44			14 48	
—	68¾	BARE LANE	d													11 25				12 53				
—	70½	**MORECAMBE**	a						09 43		10 19			10 40		11 29			12 21	12 57			14 59	
—	75	**HEYSHAM**	a													11e44							15 14	
41½	—	SETTLE	d										09 55								12 15			14 30
47½	—	HORTON-IN-RIBBLESDALE	d																		12 27			
52¼	—	RIBBLEHEAD	d																		12 36			
58¼	—	DENT	d																		12 46			
61¾	—	GARSDALE	d																		12 52			
71½	—	KIRKBY STEPHEN	d																		13 07			
82¼	—	APPLEBY	a	04 34									10 44				12 02				13 18			15 19
		APPLEBY	d	04 37			07 30						10 45				12 05				13 19			15 20
85¼	—	LONG MARTON	d				07 35														13 24			
88¼	—	NEW BIGGIN	d				07 42														13 31			
89¾	—	CULGAITH	d				07 45														13 34			
93¼	—	LANGWATHBY	d				07 51														13 40			
94¾	—	LITTLE SALKELD	d				07 55														13 44			
97¾	—	LAZONBY & KIRKOSWALD	d				08 02														13 50			
103¼	—	ARMATHWAITE	d				08 11														13 59			
113	—	**CARLISLE**	a	05b13			08 25						11 19				12 40				14 13			15 53

Heavy figures denote through carriages;
light figures denote connecting services
For general notes see page 2

For complete service between Leeds, Bradford and Keighley see Eastern Region tables; between Bare Lane, Morecambe and Heysham see Table 54

- **A** London Euston to Glasgow Central
- **B** 13 June to 5 September
- **C** Sheffield to Glasgow Central
- **D** 18 July to 5 September
- **E** 13 June to 5 September. Sheffield to Glasgow Central
- **G** 25 July to 5 September
- **H** Not Tuesdays, Thursdays and Saturdays 27 June to 19 September
- **J** 27 June to 19 September. Ship dep. Heysham 15 50 Dun Laoghaire arr. 22 40
- **K** London St. Pancras to Glasgow Central

- **b** On Mondays arr. 05 19
- **c** Not Saturdays 13 June to 5 September
- **e** 29 June to 5 September. Also Fridays and Saturdays 22 May to 27 June and 11 to 26 September. Ship dep. Heysham 12 30, Belfast arr. 19 35
- **f** Saturdays only

Carlisle has been withdrawn. The following stations have been closed: Horton-in-Ribblesdale, Ribblehead, Dent, Garsdale, Kirkby Stephen, Long Marton, New Biggin, Culgaith, Langwathby, Little Salkeld, Lazonby & Kirkoswald, Armathwaite. The area is served by buses operated by Ribble Motor Services Limited, Hillcrest Coaches, G. N. E. Motor Services.' The supplement then went on to detail the amended and withdrawn services.
Peter Waller collection

Table 76

Weekdays

Leeds to Skipton, Heysham and Carlisle

													SX				A
LEEDS CITY d	13 50	..	14 52	..	15 35	..	..	16 05	..	17 12	..	17 39	..	18 10	..	19 13	..	20 24	..	21 08	..
BRADFORD FORSTER SQUARE d	13 47	..	14 47	..	15 40	..	..	..	..	17 18	..	17 43	..	17 55	..	18b50	..	19 55	..	21c00	..
SHIPLEY d	14 09	..	15 11	..	15 56	..	..	16 25	..	17 34	..	18 00	..	18 29	..	19 32	..	20 43	..	21c06	..
BINGLEY d	14 16	..	15 18	..	16 03	..	..	16 32	..	17 41	..	18 07	..	18 36	..	19 39	..	20 50	..	21 29	..
KEIGHLEY a	14 22	..	15 24	..	16 09	..	..	16 38	..	17 47	..	18 13	..	18 42	..	19 45	..	20 56	..	21 36	..
d	14 24	..	15 26	..	16 11	..	..	16 39	..	17 48	..	18 15	..	18 43	..	19 46	..	20 57	..	21 39	..
SKIPTON a	14 36	..	15 38	..	16 23	..	..	16 51	..	18 00	..	18 27	..	18 55	..	19 58	..	21 09	..	21 51	..
d	14 38	..	..	..	16 25	16 33	..	..	..	18 02	..	..	..	..	..	..	..	..	..	21 53	..
GARGRAVE d	14 45	..	..	..	16 32	16 40	..	..	..	18 09	..	..	..	..	..	..	..	..	..	..	..
HELLIFIELD d	14 56	..	..	..	16 43	16 51	..	..	..	18 20	..	..	..	..	..	..	..	..	..	22 09	..
LONG PRESTON d	14 59	..	..	..	16 46	16 54	..	..	..	18 23	..	..	..	..	..	..	..	..	..	..	..
GIGGLESWICK d	15 06	..	..	..	16 53	..	..	..	..	18 30	..	..	..	..	..	..	..	..	..	..	..
CLAPHAM (YORKS) d	15 16	..	..	..	17 03	..	..	..	..	18 40	..	..	..	..	..	..	..	..	..	..	..
BENTHAM d	15 22	..	..	..	17 09	..	..	..	..	18 46	..	..	..	..	..	..	..	..	..	..	..
WENNINGTON d	15 27	..	..	..	17 14	..	..	..	..	18 51	..	..	..	..	..	..	..	..	..	..	..
CARNFORTH a	15 41	..	..	..	17 28	..	..	..	..	19 05	..	..	..	..	..	..	..	..	..	22 44	..
d	15 43	..	..	..	17 30	..	..	..	..	19 07	..	..	..	..	..	..	..	..	..	22 45	..
BARE LANE d	..	..	..	..	17 39	..	..	..	..	19 16	..	..	..	..	..	..	..	..	..	..	..
MORECAMBE a	15 57	..	..	..	17 43	..	..	..	..	19 20	..	..	..	..	..	..	..	..	..	22 57	..
HEYSHAM a	..	..	..	..	..	..	..	..	..	..	..	..	..	..	..	..	..	..	..	23 12	..
SETTLE d	..	..	..	..	..	17 01	..	..	..	..	..	..	..	..	..	..	..	..	..	..	..
HORTON-IN-RIBBLESDALE d	..	..	..	..	..	17 13	..	..	..	..	..	..	..	..	..	..	..	..	..	..	..
RIBBLEHEAD d	..	..	..	..	..	17 22	..	..	..	..	..	..	..	..	..	..	..	..	..	..	..
DENT d	..	..	..	..	..	17 32	..	..	..	..	..	..	..	..	..	..	..	..	..	..	..
GARSDALE d	..	..	..	..	..	17 38	..	..	..	..	..	..	..	..	..	..	..	..	..	..	..
KIRKBY STEPHEN d	..	..	..	..	..	17 57	..	..	..	..	..	..	..	..	..	..	..	..	..	..	..
APPLEBY a	..	..	..	..	..	18 08	..	..	..	..	..	..	..	..	..	..	..	..	..	..	..
d	..	..	..	..	..	18 10	..	..	..	..	..	..	..	..	..	..	..	..	..	..	..
LONG MARTON d	..	..	..	..	..	18 15	..	..	..	..	..	..	..	..	..	..	..	..	..	..	..
NEW BIGGIN d	..	..	..	..	..	18 22	..	..	..	..	..	..	..	..	..	..	..	..	..	..	..
CULGAITH d	..	..	..	..	..	18 25	..	..	..	..	..	..	..	..	..	..	..	..	..	..	..
LANGWATHBY d	..	..	..	..	..	18 31	..	..	..	..	..	..	..	..	..	..	..	..	..	..	..
LITTLE SALKELD d	..	..	..	..	..	18 35	..	..	..	..	..	..	..	..	..	..	..	..	..	..	..
LAZONBY & KIRKOSWALD d	..	..	..	..	..	18 41	..	..	..	..	..	..	..	..	..	..	..	..	..	..	..
ARMATHWAITE d	..	..	..	..	..	18 50	..	..	..	..	..	..	..	..	..	..	..	..	..	..	..
CARLISLE a	..	..	..	..	..	19 04	..	..	..	..	..	..	..	..	..	..	..	..	..	..	..

Heavy figures denote through carriages; light figures denote connecting services
For general notes see page 2

For complete service between Leeds, Bradford and Keighley see Eastern Region tables; between Bare Lane, Morecambe and Heysham see Table 54

A Ship dep. Heysham 23 45 Belfast arr. 06 50
MX and Sundays

b On Saturdays dep. 19 05
c Change at Keighley

Carlisle, Heysham and Skipton to Leeds

Miles	Miles			A					B MX		MO		C SO									D SO		E SO
0		**CARLISLE**	d	**01 33**																**08 35**				
9¾	—	ARMATHWAITE	d																	**08 52**				
15¼	—	LAZONBY & KIRKOSWALD	d																	**09 01**				
18¼	—	LITTLE SALKELD	d																	**09 08**				
19¾	—	LANGWATHBY	d																	**09 13**				
23¼	—	CULGAITH	d																	**09 19**				
24¾	—	NEW BIGGIN	d																	**09 24**				
27¾	—	LONG MARTON	d																	**09 30**				
30¾	—	APPLEBY	a																	**09 36**				
			d																	**09 38**				
41½	—	KIRKBY STEPHEN	d																	**09 57**				
51¼	—	GARSDALE	d				**06 46**													**10 16**				
54¾	—	DENT	d				**06 52**													**10 22**				
60¾	—	RIBBLEHEAD	d				**07 01**													**10 31**				
65½	—	HORTON-IN-RIBBLESDALE	d				**07 08**													**10 38**				
71½	—	SETTLE	d				**07 16**													**10 46**				
—	0	**HEYSHAM**	d						**06 40**		**06c40**													
—	4½	**MORECAMBE**	d						**06 55**		**06 55**				**07 35**								**10 00**	**10 43**
—	6¼	BARE LANE	d												**07 39**								**10 04**	
—	10¾	**CARNFORTH**	a												**07 47**								**10 13**	**10 56**
—	—		d												**07 49**								**10 15**	**10 58**
—	20¼	WENNINGTON	d												**08 04**								**10 30**	
—	23½	BENTHAM	d												**08 11**								**10 37**	
—	27¾	CLAPHAM (YORKS)	d												**08 19**								**10 45**	
—	33½	GIGGLESWICK	d												**08 29**								**10 55**	
75¼	37	LONG PRESTON	d				**07 22**								**08 35**					**10 52**			**11 01**	
76¾	38½	HELLIFIELD	d				**07 26**		**07 44**		**07 44**				**08 39**					**10 56**			**11 05**	
83	44¾	GARGRAVE	d				**07 35**								**08 48**					**11 05**			**11 14**	
86¾	48½	**SKIPTON**	a	**03 13**			**07 40**		**07 57**		**07 57**				**08 55**					**11 11**			**11 20**	**11 46**
			d	**03 18**	**07 00**	**07 30**	**07 48**		**08 00**		**08 00**		**08 12**		**08 57**		**09 33**		**10 14**			**11 15**	**11 22**	**11 48**
96	57¾	KEIGHLEY	a		**07 12**	**07 42**	**08 00**		**08 12**		**08 12**		**08 24**		**09 09**		**09 45**		**10 26**			**11 27**	**11 34**	**11 58**
			d		**07 13**	**07 43**	**08 02**		**08 13**		**08 13**		**08 28**		**09 10**		**09 46**		**10 27**			**11 29**	**11 36**	**12 01**
99¼	61	BINGLEY	d		**07 18**	**07 48**			**08 18**		**08 18**		**08 33**		**09 15**		**09 51**		**10 32**			**11 34**	**11 41**	**12 08**
102¼	64	SHIPLEY	a		**07 24**	**07 54**			**08 24**		**08 24**		**08 38**		*09e26*		**09 58**		**10 38**				**11 47**	**12 14**
105	66¾	BRADFORD FORSTER SQUARE	a		*07 51*	*08 24*			*08b45*		*08 45*		**08 45**		*09e33*				*11 06*				*12 01*	**12 21**
113	74¾	**LEEDS CITY**	a	**03 50**	**07 44**	**08 14**	**08 27**		**08 45**		**08 45**				**09 37**		**10 20**		**10 58**			**11 53**	**12 07**	

Heavy figures denote through carriages; light figures denote connecting services
For general notes see page 2

For complete service between Heysham, Morecambe and Bare Lane see Table 54; between Keighley, Bradford and Leeds see Eastern Region tables

A [sleeping car symbol] Glasgow Central to London Euston

B Ship dep. Belfast 22 30 **SX** Heysham arr. 05 35 **MX**

C 13 June to 5 September. [sleeping car symbol] from Heysham dep. 06 40

D 18 July to 26 September

E 13 June to 5 September

b Not Saturdays 13 June to 5 September

c 6 July to 10 August. Ship dep. Belfast 22 30 Sundays 5 July to 9 August. Heysham arr. 05 35

e Change at Keighley

Table 76 — Weekdays

Carlisle, Heysham and Skipton to Leeds

		A SO			B SO	C ✕		D SO		SX	E	G MW FX	SX		H ✕			
CARLISLE	d	..	..	..	11 50	12 05	..	..	..	..	..	..	..	..	16 33	..	17 47	..	18 12	..
ARMATHWAITE	d														16 50				18 29	
LAZONBY & KIRKOSWALD	d														16 59				18 38	
LITTLE SALKELD	d														17 05				18 44	
LANGWATHBY	d														17 10				18 49	
CULGAITH	d														17 16				18 55	
NEW BIGGIN	d														17 21				19 00	
LONG MARTON	d														17 27				19 06	
APPLEBY	a				12 41										17 33		18 20		19 12	
	d				12 42										17 35		18 21			
KIRKBY STEPHEN	d														17 56					
GARSDALE	d														18 12					
DENT	d														18 19					
RIBBLEHEAD	d														18 28					
HORTON-IN-RIBBLESDALE	d														18 35					
SETTLE	d				13 37										18 43		19 09			
HEYSHAM	d											15 40								
MORECAMBE	d	11 55	12 15					13 55	14 17			15 55	16 45				18e15	18 30		19 40
BARE LANE	d		12 19						14 21				16 49					18 34		19 44
CARNFORTH	a	12 08	12 27			The Thames-Clyde Express		14 08	14 29			16 08	16 57					18 42		19 52
	d	12 10	12 29					14 10	14 31			16 10	16 59					18 44		19 54
WENNINGTON	d		12 44						14 46				17 14					18 59		20 09
BENTHAM	d		12 51						14 53				17 21					19 06		20 16
CLAPHAM (YORKS)	d		12 59						15 01				17 29					19 14		20 24
GIGGLESWICK	d		13 09						15 11				17 39					19 24		20 34
LONG PRESTON	d		13 15						15 17				17 45		18 49			19 30		20 40
HELLIFIELD	d		13 19						15 21				17 49		18 53			19 34		20 44
GARGRAVE	d		13 28						15 30				17 58		19 02			19 43		20 53
SKIPTON	a	12 59	13 34			13 54		14 58	15 36			17 00	18 04		19 11		19 30	19 49		20 59
	d	13 01	13 36			13 59	14 32	15 00	15 38		16 08	17 15	17 15	18 06	18 50		19 34	19 51		21 01
KEIGHLEY	a	13 11	13 48				14 44	15 10	15 50		16 20	17 27	17 27	18 18	19 02		19 44	20 03		21 13
	d	13 14	13 49				14 45	15 13	15 52		16 22	17 29	17 29	18 20	19 04		19 46	20 05		21 15
BINGLEY	d	13 21	13 54				14 50	15 20	15 57		16 27	17 34	17 34	18 25	19 09			20 10		21 20
SHIPLEY	a		14 00				14 56	15 26	16 03		16 33	17 40	17 40	18 31	19 15			20 16		21 35
BRADFORD FORSTER SQUARE	a		14 31				15 10	15 34	16b45		16 45	18 00	18 00	18 53	20c14		20 29	20 29		21 42
LEEDS CITY	a	13 42	14 22			14 28	14 35	15 20	16 23		16 53	18 00	18 00	18 55	19 35		20 08	20 36		21 39

Heavy figures denote through carriages; light figures denote connecting services.
For general notes see page 2

For complete service between Heysham, Morecambe and Bare Lane see Table 54; between Keighley, Bradford and Leeds see Eastern Region tables

A 18 July to 5 September
B 13 June to 5 September. 🚢 Glasgow Central to Sheffield
C 🚢 Glasgow Central to London St. Pancras
D 25 July to 5 September
E Not Tuesdays, Thursdays and Saturdays 27 June to 19 September
G 27 June to 19 September. Ship dep. Dun Laoghaire 08 00 Heysham arr. 14 50
H 🚢 Glasgow Central to Sheffield

b On Saturdays arr. 16 36
c 8 June to 4 September
e 29 June to 5 September. Also Fridays and Saturdays 22 May to 27 June and 11 to 26 September. Ship dep. Belfast 10 30, Heysham arr. 17 35

Famous as the location where seven pre-Grouping companies met prior to 1923, Carlisle was the northernmost point reached by the Midland Railway in England. Recorded at Carlisle with the Up 'Waverley' on 17 June 1959 is 'Jubilee' No 45569 *Tasmania*. The origins of the 'Waverley' lay with the pre-war 'Thames-Forth', which had been introduced by the LMS in September 1927; suspended during World War 2, it was not until June 1957 that the St Pancras to Edinburgh service via Leeds and the line via Hawick to Edinburgh was named the 'Waverley'. The service ceased to operate during the winter months in 1964 and was withdrawn entirely in September 1968; its demise pre-dated the final closure of the ex-North British line through Hawick by some three months. Allocated to Carlisle Upperby when pictured here, No 45569 was withdrawn in May 1964 and scrapped at Crewe the following month.
Alexander McBlain/Online Transport Archive

On 16 June 1960 Class 2P No 40685 is pictured departing from Carlisle with the 4.37pm service to Bradford Forster Square. Completed at Derby in April 1932 to a design of Henry Fowler, the 4-4-0, which had been reallocated to Hellifield from Nottingham in the late summer of 1956, was approaching the last year of its operational life when recorded here; it was withdrawn in early July 1961.
Alexander McBlain/Online Transport Archive

The northernmost point of the MR's network in England was at Petteril Bridge Junction, in Carlisle, where the S&C met the existing NER line from Newcastle for the final run into Carlisle station. On 9 July 1961, the West Riding Branch of the RCTS organised the 'Borders Rail Tour' from Leeds. The train was brought from Leeds behind a Stanier Pacific – No 46247 *City of Liverpool* (see page 60) – but at Petteril Bridge Junction the 4-6-2 was replaced by a pair of Class B1 4-6-0s – Nos 61242 *Alexander Reith Gray* and 61290 – for the onwards journey through Carlisle and on to Hawick over the ex-NBR Waverley route.
John McCann/Online Transport Archive

In order to accommodate the locomotives that it used on the S&C, the MR constructed a locomotive shed – Durran Hill – on the south side of the line about half-a-mile east of Petteril Bridge Junction. The shed opened with the introduction of freight traffic over the line in August 1875 and comprised a single roundhouse along with a small repair shop. The shed was closed by the LMS on 16 February 1936 with its 27 locomotives reallocated and its duties split between Kingmoor and Upperby sheds but was reopened, as a wartime measure, in 1943. It continued in use as a store and servicing point until final closure came on 2 November 1959. The building was demolished six years later. Pictured outside the shed on 30 September 1951 are Nos 41972 and 41974; these were two of the final batch of 4-4-2Ts built to Whitelegg's original design for use on the London, Tilbury & Southend route; the arrival of Stanier's 2-6-4Ts in the mid-1930s saw the 4-4-2Ts transferred to other duties and, at Nationalisation, both Nos 41972 and 41974 were based at Dundee. Reallocated to Skipton later in 1948, both were withdrawn during 1955.
Peter Gray/Transport Treasury

There were a considerable number of industrial sidings along the line; one of these was situated between Cumwhinton and Cotehill stations where sidings were provided for the traffic from the Cocklake works of what became ultimately British Gypsum (it had previously been Howes Plaster Works and then the Carlisle Plaster Co). From the sidings, a short one-mile branch provided a connection through to the works itself. The sidings were controlled by the Howe & Cos Siding box; this had been first commissioned shortly after the opening of the line following agreement between the MR and John Howe & Co to open a siding, but had been replaced by a new MR Type 4A box in 1916 (the current 30-lever frame was installed in 1943 when the sidings were expanded to accommodate the additional traffic as a result of wartime demand). In order to operate its branch, the company employed a number of Andrew Barclay-built steam engines. The oldest of these – Works No 1147 – was 0-4-0ST *John Howe*, which was delivered in 1908 and this locomotive is pictured approaching the sidings on 3 June 1967. Steam operation ceased in the late 1960s but *John Howe* was preserved – as was the later *J. N. Derbyshire* (of 1929) – and both are now based at the Ribble Steam Railway. The gypsum mine closed, as it was worked out, on 20 July 1966 although the factory continued in production, with its raw material brought in, until the early 1980s when it closed. The branch succumbed at the same time.
Derek Cross

Heading through Armathwaite Gorge on 4 June 1966 with an Up special sponsored by the LCGB – the 'Fellsman' – are two of the celebrity 'Jubilees': No 45593 *Kolhapur* and 45596 *Bahamas*. The two 4-6-0s had taken charge of the special at Quintinshill for the return journey south as far as Crewe, where they were replaced by Nos D302 – acting as pilot for the diversionary run via Bescot to Rugby – and E3174 that took the train back to Euston. Based at Holbeck from April 1965, No 45593 was one of the octet that survived into 1967. Maintained to a high standard, No 45593 was used on specials on the S&C prior to its withdrawal in October 1967. Preserved in early 1968, the locomotive is at the time of writing based out of service at Tyseley. No 45596 was latterly based at Stockport Edgeley from where it was withdrawn in July 1966 – shortly after the date of this excursion – and was acquired for preservation in the following January. Based for many years at Dinting, No 45596 moved to the Keighley & Worth Valley Railway where it remains at the time of writing in an operational condition. *Derek Cross*

On 12 June 1967 one of the former Crosti-boilered Class 9F 2-10-0s – No 92025 – is pictured alongside the signalbox at Armathwaite having failed with a southbound goods. The MR signalbox was opened on 16 July 1899 and abolished on 15 January 1983. Whilst still owned at the time of writing by Network Rail, the box has been leased to the Friends of the Settle Carlisle Line since 1992 and has been fully restored to its original MR condition. No 92025 was one of 10 of the class – Nos 92020-29 – that were constructed at Crewe between March and July 1955 and which were equipped with the Franco-Crosti design of boiler. However, the modified design did not prove to be a success – largely as a result of corrosion – and all ten were modified to a more standard form between 1959 and 1961. When recorded here the locomotive was allocated to Birkenhead Mollington Street from where it was withdrawn in November 1967. The new order is also recorded as Brush Type 4 – No D1825 – passes through with the Up 'Midday Scot', which had been diverted away from its usual route over the West Coast main line via Shap. The Type 4 – renumbered 47344 in March 1974 – was at the time it was pictured here allocated to the Derby Division. Freight facilities were withdrawn from Armathwaite on 6 April 1964 and the track has already been rationalised.
Derek Cross

On 7 June 1955 Ivatt-designed 2-6-0 No 43049 is pictured arriving at Armathwaite station with a Down service towards Carlisle. The station – constructed to the designs of the MR's architect John Holloway Sanders – was opened with the line on 1 May 1876. Closed on 5 May 1970, the station was reopened on 14 July 1986; however, by that date, the main station building had been sold off and converted into a private house. As a result, a new shelter was constructed for use of passengers heading towards Carlisle. Completed at Horwich Works in November 1949, the Mogul was allocated to Derby when recorded here; it was transferred to Saltley in mid-1956 and then to Heaton Mersey six years later. A final move brought the locomotive to Carlisle Kingmoor in late 1964 from where it was withdrawn in August 1967.
Neville Stead Collection/Transport Treasury

Also recorded at Armathwaite on 7 June 1955 was rebuilt 'Royal Scot' No 46115 *Scots Guardsman* on an Up freight. In the background can be seen the station's goods yard; freight facilities were withdrawn from Armathwaite on 6 April 1964. The 'Royal Scot' – now one of two to survive in preservation – was originally completed by North British in September 1927. It was to achieve fame when it was used in the classic film *Night Mail* shortly after it had been equipped with smoke deflectors. Rebuilt in 1947 with a new tapered boiler, No 6115 was the only rebuilt 'Royal Scot' to operate with smoke deflectors prior to Nationalisation. Allocated to Longsight between September 1949 and September 1960, from May 1961, when it was transferred from Crewe North to Carlisle Upperby, No 46115 was to spend the bulk of its remaining mainline career based at either Upperby or Kingmoor except for a brief two-month sojourn at Wigan Springs Branch in the late spring of 1964. Withdrawn in December 1965, the locomotive was initially preserved on the Keighley & Worth Valley Railway. Based at Carnforth at the time of writing, No 46115 is mainline certified for use on steam specials.

Neville Stead Collection/Transport Treasury

The descent towards Armathwaite station incorporates three short tunnels – Baron Wood No 1 (207 Yards), Baron Wood No 2 (251 Yards) and Armathwaite (325 yards) – and on 4 June 1967 'Peak' No D57 is pictured emerging from the third of these with a Down ECS working towards Carlisle. When recorded here, the locomotive was relatively new, having been completed at Crewe Works in June 1963 and was allocated to the Leicester Division at the time. Renumbered 45042 in December 1974, the 'Peak' was to remain in service until April 1985.
Derek Cross

Recorded from the footplate of a Down service from Birmingham via Leeds to Glasgow, the train is pictured approaching the southern of the two tunnels at Barons Wood on 26 August 1967. The locomotive is 'Jubilee' No 45562 *Alberta*; this was one of the celebrity members of the class allocated to Leeds Holbeck and was destined to become the last of the class – on 4 November 1967 – to be taken out of service. Earlier that year, No 45562 had been the last steam locomotive to haul the royal train when it provided the motive power between York and Nidd Bridge. Sadly, although other examples of the class survived in preservation, there was to be no reprieve for No 45562, which was scrapped by Cashmores at Great Bridge during May 1968.
Derek Cross

Pictured from the footplate of the locomotive, Class 9F No 92056 is pictured at Long Meg Sidings with the stock for the Long Meg to Widnes anhydrite train on 15 June 1967. Anhydrite is a form of gypsum (calcium sulphate) that lacks water There is also a hydrated form and both were found in quantities in the Eden Valley although the hydrated form had a greater number of uses and the anhydrite version was, for many years, largely considered to be a waste product. However, the use of the substance in the production of sulphuric acid developed and thus generated a considerable amount of traffic for the line to take the anhydrite to the various chemical works – such as that at Widnes – that grew up during the interwar years. Visible in the distance is Ivatt Class 4 2-6-0 No 43029 with the Appleby to Carlisle pick-up freight.
Derek Cross

Pictured on 19 May 1964 is the station at Little Salkeld. Typical of the designs produced for the line by John Holloway Sanders, Little Salkeld station was closed following the withdrawal of stopping services over the line on 4 May 1970; however, unlike most of the other intermediate stations on the line that closed on that date, Little Salkeld was not reopened in 1986. The main station building, which was situated on the Leeds-bound platform, remains intact and is now a private residence.
Neville Stead Collection/Transport Treasury

Viewed looking towards the south, Langwathby station is seen here on 8 June 1965. Visible in the distance are the goods shed and signalbox. The station lost its freight facilities on 6 July 1964 but the shed, some six decades after closure, remains extant although the signalbox, which dated originally to 5 July 1903, was closed on 27 October 1968 and was subsequently demolished.
Neville Stead Collection/Transport Treasury

Viewed looking towards the north with Culgaith Tunnel in the background, Culgaith station opened on 1 April 1880. Although the buildings were again designed by Sanders, the four-year time delay resulted in Culgaith station being completed to a different style. Again closed when local services were withdrawn, Culgaith was another station that was not reopened in July 1986. The main station building, seen here, was situated on the Up platform and survives as a private residence. Part of the Up platform also survives although there is now no trace of the former Down platform and building. South of the station and across the level crossing the 16-lever MR signalbox that dates to 1908 is still extant.

Neville Stead Collection/Transport Treasury

On 11 August 1968 BR bade an official farewell to main-line steam with the operation of the 'Fifteen Guinea' special. The train operated from Liverpool Lime Street to Carlisle via Manchester and the Settle-Carlisle route. Having arrived 33 minutes late on the outbound trip – reaching Carlisle at 3.29pm – the return working departed 14 minutes late at 3.44pm. For the first section of the return leg, the train was hauled by two Class 5 4-6-0s – Nos 44871 (pilot) and 44781 – for the run back to Manchester Victoria. The pair is seen heading south at Culgaith. Although No 44781 was scrapped in December 1968, No 44871 was preserved. *Derek Cross*

Recorded at New Biggin on 15 June 1967 '9F' No 92056 is pictured with the Long Meg to Widnes anhydrite train. Visible in the distance is New Biggin signal box; this opened in 1890 and closed on 16 December 1973.
Derek Cross

With the junction that provided the link between the Midland and North Eastern lines at Appleby in the distance, Holbeck-allocated rebuilt 'Royal Scot' No 46133 *The Green Howards* is seen at Appleby in July 1951 with a Down service towards Carlisle. At this dated the station was still known simply as Appleby; it would not acquire the 'West' suffix – to differentiate it from the ex-NER Appleby East – until 1 September 1952. The 'Royal Scot' was to remain based at Holbeck until it was reallocated to Kentish Town in mid-October 1958. Following the rationalisation of the ex-NER route, the remaining section of the line was accessed via the link between the two routes in Appleby; the final traffic – to the Ministry of Defence base at Warcop – ceased in 1989. The junction is still in place and the signalbox has recently undergone a major refurbishment. The section of line northwards from Warcop towards Appleby is now preserved by the Eden Valley Railway Trust.
Neil Davenport/Online Transport Archive

Two decades on – on 20 September 1970 – although the infrastructure at Appleby remains remarkable unchanged there has been a dramatic alteration to the motive power used. Pictured heading southbound with the 1.48pm service for St Pancras is 'Peak' No 27. Completed at Derby in April 1961, when recorded here the 'Peak' was allocated to Leeds Holbeck shed and so would have been a regular performer over the Settle & Carlisle. It remained based at Holbeck until October 1977, having been renumbered 45028 under the TOPS scheme in February 1975, when a final transfer saw it move to Tinsley, from where it was withdrawn in December 1980 – after less than two decades of use. *Neil Davenport/Online Transport Archive*

On 5 September 1959 the crew of '8F' No 48158 is busy replenishing the tender prior to ascending towards Ais Gill at Appleby. Built at Crewe Works in January 1943, No 48158 proudly displays its 55A – Holbeck – shedplate. The locomotive was transferred to Holbeck from Nottingham in February 1948 and was to spend the rest of its operational career based there. It was withdrawn in the late summer of 1967.
Neil Davenport/Online Transport Archive

On 3 September 1954 4-6-0 No 45126 is recorded in Appleby station with a Down express. The footbridge was installed in 1901 but the main span dates to the following year, when it replaced the original which had been damaged in an accident. Historically, this was the only station on the line that was equipped with a footbridge. The Class 5, built by Armstrong Whitworth in May 1935, was allocated to Carlisle Kingmoor for its entire operational career post-Nationalisation; it was withdrawn in May 1967.
Neil Davenport/Online Transport Archive

On 7 August 1952 the Down 'Thames-Clyde Express' is pictured approaching Appleby station behind rebuilt 'Royal Scot' No 46109 *Royal Engineer*. The service, which was originally named by the LMS in 1927 and revived after World War 2, was one of the principal express trains to operate over the line. When recorded here, the express's northern terminus was Glasgow St Enoch; following closure of that station in 1966, the service was diverted to Central. The name was carried on the train until 1974 but the service lasted for a further two years. When recorded here the 4-6-0, which was one of the first nine of the type to be rebuilt (during 1943), was allocated to Holbeck shed. Apart from a brief stay at Low Moor – between September 1961 and June 1962 – Holbeck was the locomotive's home for the entire period of BR ownership; No 46109 was withdrawn in December 1962.
Neil Davenport/Online Transport Archive

Recorded passing the Express Diary sidings at Appleby, which were situated half-a-mile south of the station, on a test train on 29 August 1956 is prototype 'Deltic' No DP1 (the official designation but never actually carried by the locomotive). Built by English Electric at Preston and completed in 1955, the locomotive was fitted with two Napier Deltic E158 D18-12 motors (these are slightly different to the E169 D18-25B units fitted to the production batch built for the East Coast main line). As a result of its initial operation, 'Deltic' was modified before undergoing tests on the Settle & Carlisle during August and September 1956. The London Midland Region decided not to take the 'Deltic' project further but a modified design was subsequently adopted for use on Anglo-Scottish services to and from King's Cross. Withdrawn in November 1960 as a result of a severe oil leak, the prototype was donated to the Science Museum in 1963; transferred to the National Railway Museum in 1993, the locomotive is at the time of writing based on the Ribble Steam Railway near its Preston birthplace.
Neil Davenport/Online Transport Archive

On 9 September 1959 Class 5 4-6-0 No 45329 was employed shunting the Express Dairy sidings at Appleby. The Express Dairy creamery at Appleby dated to 1931 and the sidings were extended in 1935. Latterly, much of the milk brought into the site was for cheese production. The sidings were controlled by a ground frame, released from Appleby West, which was closed in 11 January 1970. One of the class built by Armstrong Whitworth (in March 1937), the 'Black Five' had been transferred from Upperby to Kingmoor some two months prior to being recorded here. It was not to remain at Kingmoor for long, however, as by mid-June 1960 it had been reallocated to Lancaster Green Ayre. Over the next three years it was to be transferred a further six times before it was finally withdrawn from Speke Junction, where it had been based since September 1963, in November 1966.
Neil Davenport/Online Transport Archive

Whilst the majority of stations on the line remained open until the withdrawal of local passenger services in May 1970, there were a handful that closed earlier. One of these was Crosby Garrett, which lost its passenger services on 6 October 1952. Passing the site of the closed station on 24 June 1962 with a Down freight is 'Crab' No 42771. Originally numbered 13071 when completed to a design of George Hughes at Crewe Works in July 1927, the locomotive was renumbered 2771 in August 1934. London based – at Kentish Town or Cricklewood – from early 1948, the locomotive was transferred to Holbeck – its final shed – in the late summer of 1954. When recorded here, the 2-6-0 was approaching the end of its operational life; it was withdrawn in November 1963.
Neville Stead Collection/Transport Treasury

Recorded heading south near Crosby Garrett with an Up freight on 22 July 1961 is Class 8F No 48703. One of the class built by the Southern Railway – at Brighton Works in June 1944 – during World War 2, the 2-8-0 was, when recorded here, allocated to Stourton shed in Leeds. Based there for more than a decade, the locomotive was reallocated to Royston in January 1967 from where it was withdrawn eight months later.
Neville Stead Collection/Transport Treasury

Class 4F 0-6-0 No 44183 has just crossed Smardale Viaduct and is heading south with an Up freight towards Leeds on 4 September 1954. Allocated to Carlisle Kingmoor for the entire period of its life in BR ownership, No 44183 was originally completed at St Rollox Works, Glasgow, in March 1925. It was to achieve almost 40 years of service before withdrawal in October 1963.
Neil Davenport/Online Transport Archive

Pictured approaching Smardale Viaduct on 4 September 1954 is an express from St Pancras to Edinburgh. Double-headed by two ex-LMS 4-6-0s, the lead locomotive is 'Jubilee' class No 45711 *Courageous*. At the time that the train was recorded, the 'Jubilee' was allocated to Corkerhill shed in Glasgow. The last decade of the locomotive's life saw it based in Scotland – either at Corkerhill or at Polmadie – before its withdrawal at the end of December 1962. Prior to moving to Scotland, it had spent four years based at Farnley Junction in Leeds.
Neil Davenport/Online Transport Archive

Having just passed under the road overbridge that takes the A685 over the railway the unique Class 5 No 44767 enters Kirkby Stephen West station from the north. Completed at Crewe Works in December 1947, the 'Black Five' was the only member of the class to be fitted with outside Stephenson link motion valve gear; normally fitted inside the frames of a locomotive, the last time that Stephenson valve gear had been used outside was on a GWR-built single in 1884. Although undated, the photograph probably postdates December 1964 as it was towards the end of the locomotive's career that it was reallocated to Carlisle Kingmoor having spent the bulk of its life based at Bank Hall. Withdrawn in December 1967, No 44767 was initially destined for the scrapyard but was rescued for preservation (albeit without its original tender, which had been already disposed of). At the time of writing, No 44767 is based at Carnforth where it is currently out of service.
Neville Stead Collection/Transport Treasury

Skipton-based Class 4F 0-6-0 No 44277 is pictured heading homewards with an Up freight as it passes through Kirkby Stephen West station. The station is located about 1½ miles from Kirkby Stephen itself. Initially called Kirkby Stephen when it opened on 1 May 176, it became Kirkby Stephen & Ravenstonedale on 1 October 1900 and Kirkby Stephen West (to differentiate it from the older ex-NER station) on 8 June 1953; the 'West' suffix was dropped on 6 May 1968 following the closure of Kirkby Stephen East on 2 January 1962. Closed in May 1970, Kirkby Stephen reopened in July 1986. The '4F' was new from Derby Works in December 1926 and was to be based at Skipton throughout the BR era. It was withdrawn in May 1965.
Neville Stead Collection/Transport Treasury

The view towards the south at Kirkby Stephen on 4 September 1954 shows to good effect the juxtaposition of the goods shed and signalbox. Freight facilities were withdrawn from the station almost exactly a decade after this photograph was taken – on 28 September 1964 – but almost six decades after closure, the building is still extant. The ex-Midland Railway signalbox is, however, no more; it was replaced by an LMR Type 15 box with a 20-lever frame in 1974.
Neil Davenport/Online Transport Archive

An Up service from Edinburgh to St Pancras double-headed by two 4-6-0s approaches the summit of the line at Ais Gill on 7 September 1954. Since passing Appleby, almost 20 miles to the north, the train has been climbing for virtually the entire distance, with the gradient over much of the section being 1 in 100. Once the summit has passed, the crews – in particular the firemen – will be enjoying the benefit of the long descent from Ais Gill towards Settle Junction.
Neil Davenport/Online Transport Archive

Pictured passing Ais Gill box with a Down service on 19 May 1961 is 'Black Five' No 44943. The signalbox dated to 26 April 1890 and replaced an earlier structure; closed on 28 January 1981, the box was dismantled and reconstructed to serve Butterley at the Midland Railway Centre. Based in Leeds for its entire career in BR ownership – at either Holbeck or Farnley Junction (between September 1963 and November 1966) – Horwich-built No 44943 was finally withdrawn in October 1967.
Neville Stead Collection/Transport Treasury

Pictured crossing the Dandry Mire Viaduct with an Up freight on 6 July 1950 is Class 8F 2-8-0 No 48547. The viaduct, which is situated just to the north of Garsdale station, is some 730ft in length. When the line was being constructed, the original plan was to cross Dandry Mire Moss on a long embankment. However, despite depositing some 250,000 cubic yards of material to create the embankment (which had the effect of displacing the peat to form 15ft high ridges either side of the proposed line), the bog – and the persistent rain – led to a change of plan. In place of the embankment, a viaduct – designed by John Sanders – was decided upon with construction commencing in 1873. Originally planned to incorporate eight arches, the structure as built had 12 spans; it was completed in May 1875.
Neil Davenport/Online Transport Archive

With the MR line towards Garsdale heading off to the west, ex-North Eastern Railway Class G5 0-4-4T stands in Hawes station in July 1950 with a service towards Northallerton. Work on the construction of the Hawes branch from Garsdale did not commence until the bulk of the main line had been completed. As a result, the joint station at Hawes did not open until 1 June 1878. Originally there were two signalboxes – East and West – but, in 1900, a new Hawes East box – called Hawes station after 1907 – replaced them. The signalling was maintained by the NER and its successors. The line to Garsdale closed completely on 16 March 1959 but freight traffic continued to reach Hawes from the east until facilities were withdrawn on 27 April 1964. The station remains intact with the buildings incorporated into the Dales Countryside Museum.
Neil Davenport/Online Transport Archive

Viewed from the north of Garsdale station and with the wooden fence that surrounded the turntable visible on the left, Class 4F 0-6-0 No 43893 comes off the Hawes line with an Up freight on 6 July 1950. Allocated to Skipton shed for its entire career post-Nationalisation, the '4F' would have been a regular sight travelling over the Settle & Carlisle until it was withdrawn in May 1965. *Neil Davenport/Online Transport Archive*

On 24 April 1954 the last passenger services operated on the ex-North Eastern Railway section from Northallerton to Hawes; the truncated passenger services over the route – from Garsdale to Hawes – were withdrawn on 16 March 1959. The locomotive used on the last passenger service to traverse the whole of this transpennine route was Class J21 No 65038, which carried a commemorative wreath on its smokebox. The locomotive from the train is pictured here being turned on the famous turntable at Garsdale. The wall constructed from redundant sleepers that surrounded the turntable was erected in 1900 following an incident when a heavy wind caught a locomotive on the turntable. The turntable had originally been installed in 1884 – when it cost £200 – and was to remain in situ for more than a century. It was purchased by the Keighley & Worth Valley Railway in February 1988 but, due to opposition from the Yorkshire Dales National Park Committee (which had sought to get it listed in its original location), was not installed on the preserved railway at Keighley until 1990.
Tony Wickens/Online Transport Archive

On 6 July 1950 4-6-0 No 44892 is seen entering Garsdale with a service from Carlisle to Bradford Forster Square. Garsdale was the junction for the Midland's line towards Hawes and the single-track branch can be seen heading off towards the east. The six-mile branch opened on 1 October 1878; at Hawes the line made an end-on connection with the North Eastern Railway's route through to Northallerton, which had been extended through from Leyburn. Although the Garsdale-Hawes section was owned by the MR, it was the NER that provided most of the passenger services. With the closure of the line east of Hawes in April 1954, there remained one return passenger working per day on the ex-MR section until closure on 16 March 1959. The ex-MR line closed completely from the same date; the remaining freight traffic to Hawes, until freight facilities were withdrawn in April 1964, travelled via the ex-NER line. *Neil Davenport/Online Transport Archive*

Viewed from the east on 8 September 1951, a Class G5 0-4-4T – No 67291 – stands at Garsdale station with the next service on the line towards Hawes and Northallerton. The station at Garsdale opened as Hawes Junction on 1 August 1876; it was renamed Hawes Junction & Garsdale on 20 January 1900 and did not become simply known as Garsdale until 1 September 1932. The station was closed on 4 May 1970 although it was still used by excursion trains. On 3 May 1975 it reopened for Dales Rail use in the summer but was fully reopened on 14 July 1986. The station buildings, which were designed by John Holloway Sanders, are now Grade II listed as is the signalbox. The latter, a Midland Railway Type 4C box installed in June 1910, has recently undergone a refurbishment.
Tony Wickens/Online Transport Archive

With the southern portal of the 1,213-yard long Rise Hill Tunnel in the background Stanier-designed 2-6-4T No 42654 is seen approaching Dent station with an Up service on 11 June 1960. A Bolton-allocated locomotive throughout its BR career, No 42654 is well away from its normal haunts when pictured here.
Neville Stead/Transport Treasury

Class 9F 2-10-0 No 92075 is seen at Dent with a Down freight on 31 May 1966. At 1,150ft above sea level, Dent is the highest operational railway station in England on the National Rail network. It is also, arguably, one of the most remote, being situated almost five miles to the east – and some 400ft above – the village of Dent itself. The station here opened slightly later than the line itself – on 6 August 1877 – but was closed along with most of the surviving intermediate stations on 4 May 1970 when local passenger services were withdrawn. It reopened in July 1986.

When recorded here the '9F' was a relatively recent arrival; it had been transferred from Kirkby in Ashfield to Carlisle Kingmoor just over a month prior to the date of the photograph. New in March 1956, having been completed at Crewe Works, the locomotive was initially allocated to the Great Central and its transfer away from the Midlands was as a consequence of the closure of that route. It was not to survive at Carlisle long, being withdrawn in mid-September 1966.
Neville Stead/Transport Treasury

Pictured heading northbound with a Down express on 30 July 1966 on the approach to Dent station is 'Jubilee' No 45675 *Hardy*. Allocated to Holbeck shed in Leeds throughout the BR era, No 45675 was one of only eight of the class to survive into 1967; it was finally withdrawn towards the end of June that year.
Neville Stead Collection/Transport Treasury

On 13 May 1961 'Royal Scot' No 46117 *Welsh Guardsman* is seen at the head of an Up service at Dent Head. From here the crew faces a short gradient up into Blea Moor Tunnel and then the long descent through Horton-in-Ribblesdale and Settle to Settle Junction. Allocated to sheds in the West Riding – Holbeck, Low Moor and Farnley Junction – throughout its BR career, the 4-6-0, which had been one of the first of the class to be rebuilt (during 1943), was finally to be withdrawn from Holbeck shed in November 1962.
Neville Stead Collection/Transport Treasury

Pictured towards the end of their relatively short lives, two Kingmoor-allocated Class 9Fs are seen passing at Blea Moor on 28 August 1967 with Down and Up freights. No 92051 had been reallocated to Kingmoor from Newton Heath during November 1965 but No 92058's transfer from Speke Junction to Carlisle was much more recent – less than a month before it was recorded here. Both were, however, approaching withdrawal, being taken out of service in October 1967 and November 1967 respectively. Blea Moor box – which Network Rail claims as the most remote on the system – has a 30-lever frame and was constructed by the LMS on 20 September 1941; it replaced an earlier box, which dated to 1892, that was situated on the Down side.
Neville Stead/Transport Treasury

On 19 August 1967 Two 'Black Fives' – Nos 45061 and 45080 on Down and Up freights respectively – are seen just south of the 2,629-yard long Blea Moor Tunnel – the longest on the line – with Blea Moor signalbox visible in the distance. By 1967 steam operation over the S&C was drawing to a close; both of the locomotives illustrated here were withdrawn shortly after the date of this photograph. No 45061, which had been reallocated to Kingmoor in the spring of 1963, was withdrawn during November 1967 whilst No 45080, which had been transferred to Holbeck earlier in the year, was taken out of service in October 1967.
Neville Stead/Transport Treasury

Now listed Grade II*, Ribblehead Viaduct, with its 24 spans and length of 440 yards, is one of the most spectacular railway bridges on the National Network. Like all the major structures on the S&C it was designed by the MR's chief engineer, John Sydney Crossley, and took some five years to complete. The vast workforce – some 2,300 men at its peak – required in its construction was housed in a number of shanty settlements adjacent to the site; sadly some 100 workers lost their lives during work on the viaduct. The condition of Ribblehead and the cost of its repair were factors in BR's decision to try and close the S&C; with permission refused, work – which is ongoing – to the viaduct has ensured its survival. Pictured heading a Down service over the viaduct on 12 August 1967 is 'Jubilee' No 45593 *Kolhapur*.
Neville Stead Collection/Transport Treasury

Pictured entering Ribblehead station with a Down service on 1 August 1964 is 'Black Five' No 44773. The station here was opened as Batty Green on 4 December 1876; it was renamed Ribblehead on 1 May 1877. Following closure to passenger services in May 1970, the Down platform and Ribblehead signalbox (which had closed on 17 August 1969) were both demolished in order to construct transfer sidings for a local quarry; these are still extant. When stopping passenger services were restored to the line in July 1986, Ribblehead only possessed a platform in the Up direction; it was not until 28 May 1993 that a new Down platform – located slightly to the south of that illustrated here – was opened. When recorded here, No 44773 was allocated to Edge Hill shed, from where it would be withdrawn in December 1967.
Neville Stead Collection/Transport Treasury

Viewed looking towards the north in 1953 it is easy to see why Horton-in-Ribblesdale, during the period when James M. Taylor was stationmaster between 1947 and 1959, won the award as Best Kept Station for 17 consecutive years. The station was originally known simply as Horton when it opened on 1 May 1876; it was not until 26 September 1927 that it acquired the '-in-Ribblesdale' suffix. The station was not – indeed is not – supplied with a footbridge or subway with the result that passengers wishing to cross between the two platforms must make use of a barrow crossing that is situated at the southern end of the station.
Denis Cullum/Lens of Sutton Association

Class 4F 0-6-0 No 43868 is pictured approaching Horton-in-Ribblesdale station from the south during 1953 with a Down freight. Horton signalbox, which dated to 9 August 1896, in the background was abolished on 1 May 1984 and subsequently demolished. The train is passing the sidings that served Horton quarry; these survived in use until the early 1980s but have been subsequently removed. At the start of the 20th century, some 55,000 tons of limestone was carried by train from the quarry; this represented about a third of the mineral traffic carried by the line at the time. The quarry remains active – indeed has an anticipated life that will see limestone extracted for almost a further two decades – and there are plans, as yet unfulfilled, for the restoration of the sidings to facilitate its removal by rail.
Denis Cullum/Lens of Sutton Association

On 18 May 1963 'Black Five' No 44802 is pictured approaching Settle station with a Down service. When opened on 1 May 1876 the station was known as Settle New; the suffix was dropped on 1 July 1879 following the renaming of the original Settle station (which had been renamed Settle Old with the opening of the S&C), on the line towards Morecambe, Giggleswick on 1 November 1877. Freight facilities were withdrawn from Settle on 12 October 1970 and the track south of the station was rationalised; today, there is simply double track through the two-platform station. Originally there was no footbridge at the station – passengers having to make use of a barrow crossing at the north end of the station – but one, an ex-NBR example recovered from Drem station, was installed in 1993. No 44802 was transferred from Holyhead to Carlisle Kingmoor in November 1962; it was based at Carlisle – either Kingmoor or Upperby – until a final transfer in January 1968 saw it move to Bolton, from where it was withdrawn five months later.

Neville Stead Collection/Transport Treasury

The southernmost point of the Settle & Carlisle – Settle Junction – where the line heads north from the earlier MR line westwards towards Morecambe – is controlled by Settle Junction signalbox (seen here in the early 1980s). The box, which is still operational, dates to 1913 although its 31-lever frame is a replacement that was installed in 1960. When the S&C was opened an interchange station, Settle Junction, was also opened – in October 1876 – but the traffic generated were poor and the station lasted barely a year before it was closed on 1 November 1877.
J. G. S. Smith/Transport Treasury

On 9 July 1961 the RCTS (West Riding Branch) organised the 'Borders Rail Tour' which employed Stanier Pacific No 46247 *City of Liverpool* on the outward journey from Leeds City towards Carlisle. The train stopped at Hellifield, where – as can be seen here – the locomotive took water before starting its ascent from Settle Junction northwards.
John McCann/Online Transport Archive

A busy scene at Hellifield shed on 1 July 1950 shows to good effect the railway in transition after Nationalisation. On the extreme left is Ivatt-designed 2-6-2T No 1205 still showing its original LMS number and smokebox numberplate. In the centre is 'Black Five' No 44726, which has been renumbered and has a new BR numberplate. On the right is an earlier generation of 2-6-2T – No 40183, which is receiving water – which has received its BR numberplate but which still carries 'LMS' on his tank sides. There were originally two locomotive sheds at Hellifield; however, the ex-Lancashire & Yorkshire shed closed in 1927 leaving the ex-MR shed – illustrated here – operational. Sited to the west of the station and on the north side of the line, the facility opened in 1880 and finally closed on 17 June 1963. For a period thereafter it was used to store preserved locomotives from the National Collection but was finally demolished in the 1970s.
Neil Davenport/Online Transport Archive

Skipton station viewed from the west. The original station in Skipton, opened by the Leeds & Bradford Extension Railway on 7 September 1847, was located about quarter of a mile south-east of its current location; the new station was opened on 30 April 1876 to the designs of the MR's architect Charles Trubshaw in connection with the construction of the MR's new route to Carlisle via Settle. The new station had four platforms. The station was further expanded in 1888 when two additional platforms were added for the opening of the line via Embsay to Skipton and also later served the Grassington branch. These new platforms – visible on the extreme right of this photograph – had originally been provided with awnings although, by the date of this photograph, these had been removed and the line singled. Passenger services to Grassington ceased on 22 September whilst those to Ilkley were withdrawn on 22 March. The single line remaining survives for the stone traffic from Rylstone. Trubshaw's station remains and is now listed Grade II.
John Meredith Collection/Online Transport Archive

Stone traffic – either from quarries on the S&C or from Rylstone on the former Grassington branch – has been a major feature of the freight scene at Skipton for many years. For much of the period after the demise of steam operation, the Class 25s were regularly employed on these trains and here No 25104 is seen in the yard to the west of Skipton station with a rake of loaded stone wagons. Completed as No D5254 at Derby Works in February 1964, the locomotive was renumbered as part of TOPS in April 1974. Although undated, this view must be between December 1977, when the Longsight-allocated locomotive received modified headcode boxes (with two marker lights and black blinds) and September 1982 when it was withdrawn.
John Meredith Collection/Online Transport Archive

With a DMU standing in the Ilkley line platforms on the extreme left, 'Peak' class No D49 stands at the eastern end of Skipton station awaiting departure towards Leeds via Keighley and Shipley. The headcode – 1M86 – identifies the train as the Up 'Thames-Clyde Express'. Completed at Derby Works in October 1961, the 'Peak' is recorded here prior to it receiving the name *The Manchester Regiment* in October 1965. Renumbered 45039 under the TOPS scheme in April 1975, the locomotive was allocated to Holbeck shed between October 1972 and October 1977; its final three years were spent at Tinsley, from where it was withdrawn in December 1980.

Phil Tatt/Online Transport Archive